Santa Faux

A Christmas Miracle

H. CARLTON DUKES

DEDICATION

This book is dedicated to my mother,
a woman of faith and prayer.

TABLE OF CONTENTS

ACKNOWLEDGMENTS

I am most grateful to my mother whose teachings inspired me to write this work.

A special thanks to my editor and publisher for helping to make this dream come true.

1 INTRODUCTION

T'was the week before Christmas,
And all through the house
was a gloom so saddening,
it brought tears to a mouse.

Love was still abundant.
Both in-house and out.

In spite of the dire conditions
that made you want to pout.

Yes, the year was 1996
In the City of Youwilmis.
Youwilmis, North Dakota
A city that's quite small.

Population of 20,000
And, it decreases every fall.

Take a look
inside the brick home
of Leah Hopewell
To see her daughter
- the pride and joy of her life
In a world, full of love
joy, heartache and tragedy.

Early on Monday morning,
the dogs barked as if to say:
"Thank you, Mr. Sun"
for appearing that day."

Snowfall was a by-gone conclusion
Every day.

In a city that was chilly
frigid cold on holidays.

The kids slept a little longer
because the schools were all closed
that day.

"Another snow day"
"Another snow day"
The children laughed and would
often say

"How lucky we are"
"How lucky we are"
To stay home from school
one more day.

Grabbing their boots,
coats, hats and gloves
they ran outside to play,

Riding their sleighs on makeshift
hills, their laughter filled each day.

The snowmen abounded.
Children were astounded
by sculptors of art made of snow.

The Snowball wars and frozen car
doors were the normalcy of each
frigid day.

Cars were seen sliding and some

were colliding while others were
buried in snow.

People kept slipping
and slipping and falling and
slipping through most of the day.

I prayed for their safety
and prayed for God's mercies
for laughing without shame or
delay.

Some things are too funny
to stop what you're doing
to care what others,
might think or say.

So, don't hold back or stop it!
Just laugh out and rock it!
Go ahead and be as silly as you
want to be.

For this is the season, the jubilee
season for gifts, sales, and potpourri.
So, laugh heartily....
until your laughter bring tears of joy

and enjoy this joyous moment
and truly adore.

For its better, to have laughed
than never to have laughed at all.

So, embrace this winter season
of record snowfall.

The snow, that had gathered
was now, a city matter
for the street department
workers to do!

The snow trucks were so loud
as they plowed and they plowed
unnoticed you would think
war tanks were in use.

Snow trucks, plowed and salted
and plowed and salted,
side streets & major thoroughfares.

The street department crews worked
and they worked
from morning until dust to move

mountains of snow all away.

The sunlight reflecting
off the newly fallen snow,
would blind the eyes,
with the brightness of its glow.

Christmas Day!
Christmas Day!
just six mere days away
brought excitement, hope and life
to a city in decay!

The population was depleting.
And, employment was so fleeting.

Residents kept leaving
for greener pastures in other cities

For better or for worse, the cities
diehards would vow to stay.
They kept right on believing
in spite of ....darker days.

They held onto their faith
with hope and amazing grace.

They believed
a change would come,
Even if it meant
looking…backwards and dumb.

Their children, too distracted
by all the fun in the snow.
Too busy?
Or just indifferent?
To be honest, I just don't know?
Too complicated to comprehend all
life's challenges and its woes?
Or just too busy with their friends
playing Dominoes or Tic, Tac, Toe?

Whatever the case may be,
let's take a break to see what happens
in the home of Leah Hopewell in the
Christmas novel
….**Santa Faux - The Christmas
Mystery!**

2 SOPHIA'S FAMILY

Enough of rhymes and enough of riddles let's get right down to the Novel's bits and kittles. Without further ado allow me to part as the Narrator will give you the details of how it all starts…

Sophia Hopewell *(the darling daughter of Leah Hopewell)* played with such rambunctiousness. Little did she know that her mother was dying of an incurable disease.

The doctors had given Sophia's Mom less than one week to live.

Leah was so grief stricken, that she was unable to tell her child that she was dying and would probably take her very last breath before Christmas.

Leah's mother already worked out living arrangements for little Sophia. It was their agreement that she would assume custody. Leah finished packing her suitcase for that dreaded evaluation visit to the hospice unit at the local hospital.

She now sat in the living room, rocking back and forth and back and forth, staring at family photos, as she waited for her mother to arrive and pick-up little Sophia.

Sophia was only eight years old, but very small for her size. People often mistook her to be 5 going on 6, instead of 8 1/2 going on nine.

She was a very bright child, bubbly and full of cheer and optimism. Like most children, she believed any and everything an adult would tell her, she also believed in Santa Claus.

Sophia's most prominent features were her pretty round saucer eyes, which radiantly revealed her naivety, innocence, and curiosity.

She also possessed the warmest and most enchanting smile that would make you forget about any worries or fears.

Actually, looking at Sophia, made you imagine what it must have felt like to entertain an angel unaware. Sophia was the embodiment of angelic purity and beauty in flesh.

How did she look? Well, her hair was long black and wavy, and she wore it in two ponytails.

Her complexion, caramel-colored... looking at Sophia made you think of Pocahontas – such beauty and innocence.

Her mother Leah Hopewell, was once a beautiful woman too. She was literally a grown-up version of little Sophia. However, since the diagnosis of her terminal disease six months ago, she lost so much weight that her body was now shriveled into half the person that she once was. This was the after affects from her treatments and disease complications. Her skin now clung to her bony skeleton exposing her high cheekbones and sunken eyes that was once so appealing. Her image now caused one to cringe in sympathy and to think of those starving kids you see on television from impoverished Third world countries - so frail and literally clinging to life.

In Sophia's eyes Mommy would always be Mommy – regardless of how she looked in others eyes. She still looked like beautiful Mommy to her darling little girl. Sophia smiled and looked at her mom and in the most loving way, she quickly expressed her Christmas list as if she was reading it to Santa, *"Mommy, Mommy - Christmas is next week, and I want Santa to bring me a Barbie doll and, a Barbie house, and a bicycle, and a baby pee wee, and rollerblades."*

"Baby, you know Momma is going into the hospital today and Granny is going to keep you until I get out....DING DONG....*(the doorbell rings)*...that's Granny now!

"I'll get it, I'll get it," replied Sophia hurriedly, as she ran down the hallway recklessly, in a race against herself, to see who would answer the door first.....*finishing in a tie*, she grasped the doorknob, unlocked the door and gave the handle a giant twist.

"Hi Granny!" (Granny kneeled down, picked up Sophia, and gave her a big kiss)....as Sophia hugged her neck. Granny said to Sophia, *"Are you ready to come stay with Granny?"*

Sophia spoke softly, *"Yes, but only until Momma gets out of the hospital!"*

Granny looked down at her granddaughter. Then she looked across the room' at her daughter with a confused expression! Slowly placing Sophia down, she walked over to her daughter and whispers, "You didn't tell her yet?"

"No Momma, it's so hard to accept

what the doctor said," *(as she swallowed hard to fight back tears...she whispers to her mom) –* "I'll tell her tomorrow!"

Granny smiled at Leah, ...nodding her head in approval, as she took Little Sophia's hand, picked up her suitcase, and proceeded to walk out the door. As the door closed, Leah broke down in tears, falling to her knees and cried out... "Why God?"

"....Why God?"

".....Why Me?"

Leah cried for a solid hour, *drifting in and out of consciousness,* she coiled onto the floor in the fetal position.

She finally fell asleep, only to be awakened hours later by the telephone ringing. With both eyes puffy and red and dried tears on her cheeks, she picked up the phone.....

"Hello! – Honey? this is your mother, why aren't you at the hospital? Your doctor called looking for you. You should have been there hours ago!"

I know Momma, I just couldn't bring myself to go... Momma, I'm so depressed and scared, I'm afraid, I don't want to die!....Life is so unfair! Why is this happening to me?

......Doesn't God care about my baby?

.....Doesn't he care about me?

....Why would he take me from her?

"Leah.... we've discussed this before. Sophia will be well taken care of! God is in control and God always knows what's best even

*though we may not understand
...Now pull yourself together, and
check yourself into the hospital,
okay Honey?"*

"....Alright Momma..." uttered
Leah.

The next day Granny took Sophia to
the shopping mall to visit Santa.
While sitting on Santa's lap Sophia
excitingly whispered to Santa all the
things she wanted for Christmas: *"I
want Santa to bring me a Barbie
doll and, a Barbie house, and a
bicycle, and a baby pee wee, and
rollerblades and that's all."*

Unfortunately, Granny could not
hear Sophia's whispers into Santa's
ear. As life would have it, Leah's
illness affected her memory, and she
could not remember to relay this
Christmas list to Granny before she
went shopping for Sophia's presents.

So, Granny took it upon herself to get Sophia the most popular and frequently advertised toys on the market.

3 THE HOSPITAL VISIT

Later, that day Granny and Sophia
would visit Leah at the hospital.
Upon entering the hospital, Sophia
was like a Mexican jumping bean
(jumping here and jumping there).

She was so, so excited about the
very thought of seeing and visiting
her mom!

As Granny approached the
information booth, she greeted the
attendant with a friendly, "Hello"
and gave the name Leah Hopewell
to the attendant who paused briefly

to type in the last name..."Got it, she's in the Intensive Care Unit (ICU) room number: 777A."

"Thank you," replied granny and they proceeded to board the elevator.

As the elevator drew to a stop, granny held her stomach. "*This is the floor Honey*," she said to Sophia. As they exited the elevator they noticed a strong odor of sickness in the air.

The floor was very quiet and was kept very clean. They passed the nurses station and they greeted the RN's with a warm, "Howdy!"

As they continued to walk, they passed rooms of elderly people that looked like they were ready to depart this earth at any moment... 773, 775, 777A... "*Here it is*," Granny said Sophia.

Granny stopped momentarily, to compose herself...she closed her eyes and whispered a silent prayer as she squeezed Sophia's hand ever so gently. She inhaled deeply, and forced a smile on her face as she entered the room....tiptoeing so as not to disturb Leah's rest.

When Sophia entered the room she immediately noticed all the tubes in mommy's arms and nose, right away, she became frightened and reluctant to approach her mother who was so weak that she could barely talk. Nonetheless, when Leah saw her daughter, she perked up and managed to awkwardly smile.

Leah's pink watery eyes brightened as she attempted to fight back tears which felt like a glass of water, filled to the brim, and droplets away from over flow. ..."*Hi baby, how is mommy's baby doll doing?*" Sophia smiled when she heard her mother's voice and ran to her mother's bedside wrapping her little arms around momma and her tubes.

"Be careful," (Granny blurted out) *"Or else you'll disconnect one of those there tubes."* "It's okay," muttered Leah, perking up after seeing her only child.

Sophia wasn't always the only child. Eight years ago, Leah's husband and their three children were involved in a tragic car accident that killed her husband of 20 years and their two children Michelle, age15, and Kevin, age 13. Sophia was only six months old, and she escaped injury-free. Leah was not as fortunate, she suffered a broken arm and leg, fractured ribs, and traumatic head injuries.

Leah recovered after years of surgery and therapy. Her life had not been the same since; especially after being diagnosed six months ago with AIDS, she was diagnosed with the Acquired Immune Deficiency Syndrome, after she received tainted blood from a transfusion after the car accident.

This news along with the doctor's prognosis of less than a week to live - sent her to a deep dark place she could only hope was a bad dream.

As Sophia hugged her Mom...Leah drifted off to sleep within minutes, due to the strong narcotic pain medication.

Granny and Sophia would leave moments later, expecting and hoping to see Leah several more times before the inevitable would take place.

4 WHITE CHRISTMAS

Unfortunately, later that night...a snow storm hit the small City of Youwilmis, North Dakota, dumping 24 inches of snow and ice that paralyzed the city.

A travel advisory was issued and residents were told to stay off the roads. As a result, Granny and Sophia were home bound. Their expectations and plans to spend the majority of their day at the hospital came crumbling down like a house of cards.

Granny, made up for the inconvenience caused by the unexpected weather, by calling the hospital several times a day to check on her daughter, so that Sophia could speak to her mom.

As the days went by, Granny wondered to herself, if she would get a chance to see her daughter again, in person and alive.

Days cooped up in the house, felt like weeks, especially since they were unable to visit Leah, as they had originally planned.

Christmas Eve was now upon them, and Granny knew that the inevitable was drawing ever so near. She replayed in her mind what the doctor's had told her about Leah, not making it to or past Christmas. She knew, deep down within her soul, that the bad news would eventually come sooner...than later.

In spite of the doctor's prognosis, she hoped against hope, and prayed without ceasing, that she and little Sophia would be spared any sad news of Leah's expected and anticipated departure - especially on Christmas Day.

Because Christmas represents joy and happiness! Christmas is the zenith of all the universally celebrated holidays...because it represents the culmination of a busy year of work. Yes, Christmas...the holidays of Holidays - was almost here!

Christmas is the most joyous and festive time of the year! No other holiday in the world is universally celebrated and anticipated by so many people in so many different ways.

Christmas, the holiday of Holidays with so many different meanings for so many different people.

For some, Christmas is about the miraculously mysterious inception and conception of baby Jesus being born to the Virgin Mary.

It's about the baby JESUS being born in a manger in the little town of Bethlehem.

It's about the wise men being led by a mysterious star and bringing gifts to the baby Jesus.

It's about, joy to the world, the Lord has come, let earth receive its King!

Christmas is about the birth of the Savior of the world.

To some, Christmas is Santa. It's about *Old Saint Nick*...who is better known universally as Santa Claus.

It's about Santa and his gift-making elves, his flying reindeer, and his magical flying sleigh!

It's about decorating your Christmas tree, with ornaments and lights, and putting gifts underneath your tree.

It's about house decorations inside and out. It's about shopping, cooking, Christmas music, Christmas parties, Christmas parades, snow and snowflakes, giving and gift exchange.

It's a time for family gatherings, friendly fun, fellowship, and happy memories.

Many see Christmas as a blessed time of the year, to spend quality time with family, friends and loved ones. To share, to give, to receive.

Christmas represents the time of the year to be unselfish and considerate to other less fortunate families, friends and those in need.

Yes, Christmas represents so much to so many people young and old and yet the true blessings and wonders of the Christmas season gets often overlooked or taken for granted.

Let's start with the blessing of sight ...without eyesight we would not be able to see all the beautiful Christmas decorations in our neighborhoods and beyond. Without sight we would miss the ability to visually take in all the wonderful sparkling, flashing and glittering lights that are extravagantly seen and elegantly draped on Christmas Trees, houses, buildings and other elaborate objects and figurines.

Let's not forget the blessing of hearing...the ability to hear or listen to all the beautiful sounds of Christmas music, the joyful laughter and cheerful voices, the euphoric exciting shrills of children and adults opening up presents.

And what about the ability to taste....this unique ability allows us to savor the flavor of all the specially prepared Christmas dishes, desserts and drinks…eggnog anyone?

What about the ability and blessing to smell….have you ever thought about what Christmas would be like without this important sensory? All of the wonderful aromas and fragrances of Christmas… like the Pine trees, and potpourri, the smell of burning wood on a fireplace, the smell of cookies and cakes being baked in the oven.

Our final sensory involves our ability to touch or feel. This amazing ability allows us to feel the coldness of snow when it touches our face or hands. This magnificent sensory ability of touch protects us, warns us and sometimes just informs us. Like when we feel the scorching heat, while holding a cup of hot chocolate, or when we feel the warmth and affection from a loving hug.

In addition to those five amazing senses are the priceless Christmas memories, of joy, laughter and happiness.

Christmas was never meant to be an occasion for sadness and gloom.

Christmas is the time of year to exchange your gloom and sadness for brightness and gladness.

For Granny, all she wanted was to make sure Sophia's memory of Christmas did not deviate from the joyous and glorious traditions of Christmas past.

5 THE NIGHT BEFORE CHRISTMAS

Sophia was all dressed and ready for bed in her Winnie the Pooh pajamas. Mesmerized, as she often was whenever she watched her favorite Christmas cartoons in front of the big screen television.

Sophia sat on the plush blue carpet eating popcorn, munching away, without a care in the world, and drinking her favorite soda in the cozy family room.

Granny added more wood to the fireplace in the living room which was adjacent to the family room. The day was flying by, it was now 11:00 p.m. and past the time for Sophia to go to bed.

Before being tucked into her White Oak canopy bed, she poured a tall glass of milk and placed three large chocolate chip cookies on a plate for Santa. She left them neatly arranged on the kitchen table.

Lastly, before Granny tucked her into bed, Sophia got on her knees and said her prayers. Granny, kissed her good night and said, "*Tomorrow will be Christmas*!" Sophia smiled and closed her eyes.

As Granny exited the room, she thought about her daughter Leah and the latest status she received from the nurse when she called the hospital. The nurse said that Leah was sleeping and in stable condition. She could only pray and hope that her daughter wouldn't suffer much longer. Christmas Eve was drawing to a close and Granny needed to wrap Sophia's gifts and place them under the Christmas tree.

Before doing that she decided to take a break and watch her favorite Christian network station.

Granny walked over to the light switch on the wall in the hallway and dimmed the lights, then she walked over to her favorite Lazie Boy recliner that sat slightly to the right of the Big Screen TV, as she plopped into the chair.

Sophia always laughed, anytime Granny plopped herself into that Lazie Boy recliner, because the mere sound of all the air, rapidly and forcibly leaving those poor cushions was humorous in and of itself...

...... but when you add the way
Granny just plopped in that chair,
made it such a hilarious sight to see!

6 SANTA IS HERE

It was 1:00 a.m. when Sophia was awakened by what she thought was the sound of Santa's reindeer bells.

She knew it wasn't time for her to get up....but in her mind she felt this was her best opportunity to sneak a peak of Santa leaving gifts under her Christmas tree.

As Sophia pulled back her blanket, she gingerly placed one foot after the other on the floor. Being ever so quiet, she tiptoed out of her bedroom and preceded slowly and carefully down each step of the staircase.

After what appeared like an hour
she finally reached the bottom of the
stairs.

With her heart racing and her palms
sweating, Sophia got down on her
hands and knees and began to crawl
toward the wall that was perpendicular
to the family room.

As she quickly peeked her head out
then back, she caught a glancing
glimpse of a figure in red placing gifts
under the Christmas tree.

Her heart beats got louder and
louder....the pounding in her torso
had now rapidly moved from the
center of her chest to the perimeters
of her throat, *(she tried swallowing
several times with the hope that it
would dissipate)*.

No such luck...then she tried taking
short intermittent breaths - with the
hope of silencing the loud pounding

sound by cutting off its air supply - no such luck!

Sophia's final attempt to muzzle the loud sound of her heartbeat was by holding her breath.

Unfortunately holding her breath, only moved the heartbeat sound from her throat to her eardrums and then to her head....she was sure that the LOUDNESS of her POUNDING HEART and HEAD would soon be heard by Santa and reveal her hiding place.

7 THE FILLED ROOM

Within milliseconds, the thoughts of being discovered left her mind as she heard the volume of the TV get turned higher - drowning out the loud beating of her heart and head.

She could now only hear the words of the preacher on the Christian network station talking about the true meaning of Christmas.

"The true meaning of Christmas is to celebrate the birth of Christ who was named JESUS.

JESUS the Christ or the anointed

Savior who came to save a sin sick world.

Santa is a fantasy but JESUS is reality. He is the truth and the light of the world.

Jesus is the Savior, our deliverer, he's a father to the fatherless, he's a mother to the motherless, and he's everything you will ever need.

If you need a lawyer in the court room, he's a lawyer.

If you need counseling in any area in your life, ...he's the great counselor.

If you need a friend, he's a friend to the friendless.

If you're sick and need a doctor...he's a doctor in your sick room.

If you're in need of healing, he's the healer of all healers!

He is the great I AM!

So on this early Christmas morning, is there anyone in need of forgiveness of their sins?

Is there anyone in need of healing in their body?

Perhaps you know someone in the hospital ...... on their deathbed, in need of the miraculous healing touch of JESUS, if so, ...pray with me right NOW because there is a miracle in the NOW...

In the Bible in the book of Hebrews 11:1 *(paraphrased),* "NOW faith is the substance of things hoped for the evidence of things not seen."

Beloved, your NOW faith is

critically important, just like your NOW belief is.

Also, in the Bible....in Mark 11:24, it relatively states, *"Therefore ... whatever you ask for in prayer ,...BELIEVE...that you have RECEIVED IT, and IT WILL BE YOURS."*

Now, if you believe with all your heart what the word of God says in Hebrews 11:1 and in Mark 11:24 and you're in need of a Miracle NOW!

....Not next week or next month but right NOW, ...then pray this prayer with me RIGHT NOW, ... and BELIEVE that you have RECEIVED IT in your heart and mind the very moment you ask God for it in prayer.

Repeat after me:

"Father God, I come to you in the precious name of Jesus......Lord Jesus, I acknowledge you and you alone as Lord, you are the great I AM, and I acknowledge you this very moment as the anointed Christ, the Savior of this world, the deliverer, the redeemer, the healer of all Healers!"

Lord heal that mother, that father, that boy, that girl of whatever disease, is in their body.

Father God, I plead the blood of Jesus over them and I ask that you save them, deliver them, heal them, restore them whole in the name of Jesus Christ. Amen and Amen!

My dear friend, if you said that prayer with me and believed in your heart - expect a miracle!

Beloved, JESUS is the only true and faithful reason for this Christmas season, not Santa. You can put your total trust in JESUS. He'll never leave you nor forsake you.

My children and television listeners thank you so very much for tuning in to hear the word of God...because FAITH COMETH by hearing and hearing by the WORD of God.

In closing, I do pray that everyone under the sound of my voice and under the words of God will have a blessed and prosperous Christmas Day.

Until next time...May God richly bless each one of you and keep you safe until we meet again."

As Sophia opened her eyes (*after praying*). She could see and hear Granny clapping and lifting her hands shouting,

"Hallelujah, Hallelujah, Hallelujah....Glory to God...Hallelujah"

8 THE GETAWAY

At that instance, Sophia realized that this was the perfect moment to sneak back upstairs and get back into her bed unnoticed.

She mentally and visually mapped out the escape route back to her room.

Sophia stealthily and cautiously proceeded to put her plan into action by methodically crawling on her hands and knees.

She sometimes had to resort to lying totally flat on the floor (on her stomach) crawling using only her hands and forearms to inch forward unnoticed.

Finally, Sophia reached her room after what appeared to be an hour of scooting and crawling. She was relieved, but totally exhausted.

In addition to her physical exhaustion, she was also mentally and emotionally drained from her triumphant mission of Christmas espionage and Santa Claus surveillance.

The very moment, Sophia's little head hit the pillow, she fell fast asleep. Sophia slept soundly for 8 long hours.

Sophia was finally awakened out of her slumber by the sound of Christmas music playing in the house. She immediately popped up out of bed and ran downstairs to see what gifts Santa Claus had left her.

It was now 12:00 noon and the sun was shining very brightly. This particular Christmas Day was unusually warmer than most.

The unseasonably warm weather had melted all the snow and ice off the roads and sidewalks.

The snowflakes sparkled brilliantly from the reflection of the Sun, as if they were diamond crystals. What a beautiful day! She could hardly wait to open her beautifully wrapped gifts.

As she opened gift after gift, she would jump and scream in utter excitement - saying repeatedly, *"This is what I always wanted!"*

Smiling from ear to ear, she ran throughout each room, seeking out Granny to give her a great, big, bear hug and a kiss! She also wished her a Merry Christmas!

Granny, finally located her camera, and began to take pictures of Sophia as she opened all of her remaining gifts.

The atmosphere in the house was full of love and joy, smiles and laughter, as well as life and excitement!

Granny turned on the big screen television so Sophia could watch the Christmas parade.

While Sophia was preoccupied with her toys and the parade, Granny walked into the kitchen to place a call to the hospital to check on the status of her daughter, Leah.

9 THE EMPTY ROOM

"Good afternoon, I'm calling to check on my daughter, Leah Hopewell in room 777A"

"....What?...".

"What do you mean no one is in that room?"

Granny's beautiful Christmas day was now unraveling and turning into a nightmare...

When Granny heard the nurse say that no one was in that room, she appeared to go numb all over her body, Granny was so out of sorts and stunned by the nurse's response, that she unconsciously tuned out everything that was said, afterward the words, *"Ma'am, I need to place the call on hold so I can check our records."* All granny could think was that her baby was no longer alive!

As the tears began to well up in her eyes, she knew that she could not hold them back much longer.

It would not take long before the slow trickle of a tear or two would soon give way to a down pour of tears that would overflow uncontrollably, just like a flooded river that overflows a levee.

Suddenly and unexpectedly she heard the sound of the doorbell…*"Ding dong, ding dong"* – someone was actually ringing her front doorbell on Christmas day!

Who could it be?....

10 ANGELIC VISITATION

...Ding Dong, Ding Dong, Ding Dong... *(someone was ringing the doorbell)....*

Now, this was the worst possible time for anyone to be stopping by to visit. Timing could not have been any worse.

In between watching the Christmas parade on tv and playing with her new toys, Sophia shouted out to Granny, *"The doorbell is ringing, the doorbell is ringing."*

Sophia was so mesmerized by all her new toys, the Christmas parade and the joyful holiday music in the background.

Granny did the best she could to wipe the tears from her face, but the tears kept flowing uncontrollably. She finally gained her composure, after several attempts, by inhaling and exhaling deeply, to gain her poise before heading toward the front door.

As she walked slowly down the hallway, Sophia raced to her side grasping her tear-dampened hand. Granny looked down at Sophia and smiled.

When Granny finally reached the front door, she cautiously pulled back the curtain that covered the window adjacent to the front door so as to peek to see who was outside.

The glaring rays of the sunlight made it difficult for Granny to focus through her tear soaked eyes.

She did the best she could do to make out the figures on the porch, but the sun was so bright and blinding that it distorted her vision, and made the two figures at the front door appear to be angelic beings.

Was Granny having a dream or an out of body experience? Both figures on the porch were bundled in a long hooded winter coat, with fur around their hoods.

Granny squinted her eyes again and again, but could barely see the faces of the two angelic like beings, because their hoods were so tightly wrapped around their faces.

Everything looked so surreal and dreamlike to Granny.

Her thoughts were now on Leah and the heartbreaking news from the nurse at the hospital that her baby was gone.

She tried to refocus her mind on who was at her front door but the grief and heartbreak of losing her daughter on Christmas day kept flooding her mind.

Granny wiped her tearful eyes repeatedly and took another quick look outside, doing all she could in her might to keep it all together and hold off delirium from disorientating her from reality. She appeared to notice that one of the figures seemed to have the face of her daughter Leah; in her mind's eye.

Only this face was a glow with the brightness and radiance of sun rays beaming and illuminating the outside parameters of her face. This gave the appearance that her face was glowing from the glory of God.

At that point Granny was assured in her heart and mind that she was now having an out of body experience, perhaps a dream or even an open vision or maybe Granny was just losing it and experiencing delirium?

Who knows?

Or perhaps, this was Gods merciful way of beautifully and symbolically breaking the news that Leah had successfully and peacefully transitioned from earth to glory.

This may have been God's gentle, and compassionately loving way, to help Granny accept the fact that Leah had in fact died.

If so, this gracious and merciful act of exquisite empathy from the Eternal Father, helped Granny to be at peace and strengthened during the loss of her daughter

As she stood frozen in place, she was mesmerized by the glowing beauty of her daughter's face and her glorified, raptured body!

During that momentary pause which felt like minutes, but it was more like a twinkling of an eye, Granny had a series of flashbacks about all the wonderful events that she shared with her daughter Leah.

Beginning with Leah's birth, breastfeeding her, changing her diaper, watching her sleep in her crib, picking her up in the middle of the night to stop her from crying, her first bath, her first steps, teething, her first tooth, losing her 1st tooth, her first words, combing her hair, dressing her up for church, taking her to school for the first time, teaching her to ride her bike, entering high school, graduating, getting married, and having her first child - all those sentimental events seemed to flicker through her mind like someone quickly thumbing through a book.

When Sophia tugged at her hand, Granny was jolted out of her moments of reflection.
Sophia repeatedly shouted, *"Granny, Granny, Granny...the doorbell is ringing, the doorbell is ringing! Someone's on the front porch."*

At that moment, Granny realized that she was no longer daydreaming, or seeing an open vison. As she turned to her side to acknowledge Sophia, she now refocused her attention to the front door, trying to figure out the identity of the two strange visitors.

Slowly and cautiously, she slightly cracked the door, while leaving the security chain intact to ensure their safety.

When she was only partially behind the door, she asked, *"Who is it?"*

The voice on the other side of the door replied, *"It's me, Mama!"*

Granny paused for a while. ......mystified, dazed, and discombobulated, *after hearing the voice that eerily sounded like her daughter*.

She asked once again, *"Who is it?"*

At that very moment, Granny and Sophia were perplexed, skeptical, and apprehensive.

Were they dreaming?

Was this a bad prank?

Or, was this a scheme by a would-be robber? If so, she would soon find out.

As she pondered in her mind whether to open the door or to call the police, she once again asked, *"Who is it?"*

Then, as Granny pulled the curtain back even more, but very slowly this time, she looked at the hooded figure, closest to the door.

As the figure began to look upward, Granny unexpectedly made eye contact with the *hooded stranger*.

This time Granny quickly said, *"You have the wrong house! Who are you looking for?"*

The hooded stranger replied, *"It's me, Mama......Leah!"*

Granny inhaled deeply as if the wind had been knocked out of her.

She took a second look – staring deeply into the eyes of the hooded stranger.

Without warning, Granny shouted, *"Leah, it's you! It's you!"*

Upon hearing Granny's shouting, *"It's Leah."* Sophia smiled and leaped for joy.

Granny and Sophia simultaneously screamed and shouted with excitement at the appearance of Leah.

They swung open the front door and embraced Leah with tears of joy and happiness!

As Leah walked into the house, she shouted, *"I'm healed! I'm healed! Momma....I am healed!"* The sun appeared to shine brighter and brighter at each utterance of her testimony.

Leah went on to say, *"Momma, by His stripes, I've been healed!"*

"God healed me Momma!"

"God healed me!"
As uncontrollable tears of joy streamed down her face, Sophia hugged her mother ever so tightly, bowed her head, and whispered the following Thanksgiving prayer:

Thank you JESUS for healing my Mommy!
You are truly the reason for the Season...JESUS.
You are my Christmas Miracle.
I love you Jesus!

A Christmas Poem
&
Question to Ponder

By H. Carlton Dukes

"Now after Jesus was born in Bethlehem in the days of Herod the King, Behold…Wise Men from the East came to Jerusalem saying:

"Where is He - who has been born King of the Jews?

"For we have seen his star in the East and have come to worship Him!"

What wisdom and grace
To fall on their face
To pay homage to the King of Kings
On Christmas Day! On Christmas Day! Led by the Star to thee…"[1]

'The Wise Men laid, prostrate on
the ground, to worship the Savior
and King with gifts of gold,
frankincense and myrrh
Representing his Divinity.'[2]

No gifts for Mary or Joseph
They brought only gifts to thee
Their worship and honor
Their praise and glory
Was reserved for Jesus the King

What does God think?
What would he say?
When he see's such hypocrisies of
our day?

On Christmas Day
That Wondrous Day
Take a listen to hear what he might
say: You name a day, just for me –
in honor of my birth and divinity

'But you give the praise and honor
To another instead of me..'[3]

...Idolatry, Idolatry – you practice
Idolatry instead of worship to me!

Deceptions upon Deceptions
Brainwashed to worship the beast!

Deception upon Deceptions
You justify Idolatry!

Deceived and Brainwashed
To worship the beast

'You spend and spend and worship
a tree'[4]

You choose I-dol-a-try
Over wor-ship to me

Brainwashed!
To worship the beast
Instead of the Creator
In Me!

'No Marvel, don't holler
For Satan is up to his ole tricks

Transforming into an Angel of Light
Calling himself Saint Nick!'[5]

Santa....Satan
Santa....Satan
Same letters, same name
Different spelling – rearranged

'Satan appears as an Angel of Light
Deceiving the masses
From truth and what's right'.[5]

S-a-n-t-a....S-a-t-a-n
Santa....Satan
Same letters
Same name
Different spelling
Rearranged.

"Cast out of Heaven
And hurled down to earth
Wanting to ascend above the
Heights of the clouds; he wanted to
make himself,
like the Glorified Most High"[6]

A Christmas question to ponder –
The love you share and gifts you give…..God asks, is it for me? Or is it for him?

Who are you worshipping on this day…Me or him?

Jesus Christ or Santa Claus?
Me or him?
Me or him?
Who are you truly worshipping
Me or him?

'And what is the purpose of all the sacrifices and decorations? Is it for Me or for him?'[7]

Is this a Holy day for me?
Or a Holiday for him?

Me or for him?

'Come now…it can't be for both
It can't be for both, so who are you truly worshipping -Me or him?'[8]

"For I am the Lord!
That is my Name, and my glory will
I not give to another, neither my
praise to graven images"[3]

'For I am the Lord!
That is my Name
My glory I won't share with
another'[3]

"For thou shalt worship
No other god
For the Lord whose name
Is Jealous is a Jealous God"[9]

'Awake from these vile practices
Awake from these sins
Awake from your deceptions'[10]

'Has mammon become your
friend?'[11]

Awake from your deceptions and
stop being deceived

By the customs and pagan Holiday
you practice but then claim not to
believe

Your words are so hollow
Your actions contradict

'So do what you say and say what
you believe'[12]

'Otherwise, your faith is in vain
And your walk is not in truth'[13]

'For God is seeking
True Worshippers
Who worship him in
Spirit and in Truth'[14]

Therefore we should make it our
Priority to become Worshippers
of His TRUTH!

'Not just by mere lip service
Nor by actions insincere'[15]

'Speak truth to one another
In reverence - in fear of Him.'[16]

'Love is not what you say
Love is what you do
Don't claim that you Love Him so –
When you act the way you do'[17]

Love is not what you say –
Love is what you do
'How can you say you Love God?
But hate your Brother too?'[18]

Love is not -
Just what you're claiming
Love is seen by -
What you're doing!

So don't go claiming
That you Love Him
Then turn and reject is Holy Sayings

"Work out your own salvation with
fear and trembling"[19]

But how is that even possible -
If you ignore what you're hearing?

God said in Exodus 20:3
"Thou shall have no other god's
before me."[20]

That verse makes it very clear
But some will debate and claim:
'That was the old – we're in the new
We are not under the law but living
now under Grace....'[21]

To that I say to you - Jesus made it
evidentially clear to all who trust
and believe

When he said in John 14:15
"If you Love me keep my
Commandments"[17]

Not just for today or on Christmas
Day but on each and everyday

God asks the question once again:
"Who are you truly worshipping on

Christmas Day?"

Me or him?
Me or him?

The question he inquiries from you
on this Christmas Day...

Is your worship for Me or for him?
For Me or for him?

The question you must ponder
And ask your heart and mind...is
are your Christmas actions
and sacrifices motivated
by the spirit of Jesus Christ or
by the spirit of Saint Nick?

So, look all around you
What do you see?

Does it bring me glory and worship
To me?

Now take a look outside, and tell me
what do you see?

'Are all the lights that's strung -
there to glorify me?'[4]

Now take a deeper look…
Down deep within your soul
Has your Christmas spending
Gotten out of control?

Ponder this…
What's the real reason for the
season on this special day?
And how should we celebrate
his birth on Christmas Day?

'The Wise Men worshipped
Our new born King
Bringing him gifts to reverence
His Majestic Divinity'[2]

They're our example today on how
to Worship His Divinity.
No gifts for Mary or Joseph –
They were only brought to Christ
Jesus the King.

The question you must ask
Each Christmas Day & Season
Is…Are all the things you're doing
for Christ Jesus? Or for him?

You be the judge & you be the jury
But God already knows
For its been prophesied & written

'So don't be deceived
Nor weary in well doing'[22]

'Remain faithful, watchful
constantly in prayer'[23]

'Doing all to stand, stand &
forebear'[24]

'Run if you must, doing all to flee[25]
from the bondage, sins and weights
of the customs & practices
of Idolatry.'[26]

Biblical References

King James Version

1 - Matt. 2: 1-2

2 - Matt. 2: 11

3 - Isiah: 42: 8

4 - Jer. 10:1-5

5 - 2 Cor. 11:14

6 - Rev. 12:9

7 - Isiah 1:11

8 - Luke 16:13

9 - Exodus 34:14

10 - 1 Cor. 15:34

11 - Luke 16:9

12 - James 1:22

13 - 1 Cor. 15:2

14 - John 4:23

15 - Isiah 29:13

16 - Eph. 4:25

17 - John 14:15

18 - 1 John 4:20

19 - Phil. 2:12

20 - Ex. 20:3

21 - Rom. 6:14

22 - Gal. 6:9

23 - Eph. 6:18

24 - Eph. 6:13

25 - 2 Tim 2:22

26 - 1 Cor. 10:4

About the Author

H. Carlton Dukes spent his childhood in upstate New York, with dreams of writing poetry, prose, novels, and delivering the unspoken word.

As a youth, he was an avid sports enthusiast playing football, basketball and nearly every sport available in his community. He believes that sharing the Christian faith at an age appropriate level will help to develop solid moral principles in America's youth.

H. Carlton is a graduate of Niagara University and Central Michigan University As an elementary school teacher, he taught in the New York Public School System.

H. Carlton is a longtime advocate of Christian education, reading and youth advocacy.